WRITERS'

WORKSHOP

WORKBOOK

2015

BY

CHARLENE TORKELSON

INTRODUCTION

For several years I have had the great privilege of teaching a series of Writers' Workshops for those who would like to move from simply putting words on paper to the next step of publishing their work. This workbook is an outline of several topics covered in these workshops. The ideas are intended to stimulate thought and consideration for those who are interested in this process. Please use the space provided to note your own ideas and impressions, set goals, and create plans for this next step.

This is the second edition of this workbook.

Charlene Torkelson

TABLE OF CONTENTS

START AT THE BEGINNING

Most editors and published authors when asked to give advice to new writers advise them to write about that they know. So the question is what do you know?

You will find when you write about something you are familiar with, the writing process moves along quickly and smoothly. Make a list of all the topics and subjects that you feel you know best.

Start at the beginning. That means, where were you born? You might ask, "You mean I have to go THAT far back?" Yes, list the places you have lived or visited. Those are the places you will somehow represent in your writing whether it has to do with a memory of a place or a description — it will show up in your writing. Next to each place, describe something special or unique about it. Maybe it is a specific location or a business that makes that place famous. It could be a custom or tradition. Jazz is New Orleans, Broadway is New York, and movies are

Hollywood. What is special about the places you remember?

_____

_____

_____

_____

_____

_____

_____

_____

_____

_____

We are all shaped by the people we know and meet. Whether you write fiction or non-fiction, those people will be important to your writing. Make a list of these people and describe their characteristics. What makes them a part of your life? How have they influenced you?

_____

_____

_____

_____

_____

_____

_____

_____

_____

_____

_____

_____

_____

_____

_____

_____

When I began my writing career, I took a course with the first assignment to write "My Story". So I challenge you, if you have not written your story before, do it now. Try to keep the word count at 1,000 words. This is a typical word count for a magazine article. So in addition to writing about yourself, you now are limited to a typical article length. What events have shaped your life?

_____

_____

_____

New writers — and old writers — often find it difficult to find an acceptable writing topic. How do we find new ideas? Sometimes it might be from a news story, from a conversation with a friend, or from a long nagging interest. Maybe it is something that happened to you or that you witnessed that has given you an urge to put it down on paper. I once saw a story on the news about wind turbines used at the college I attended. It made me want to research further on this topic. I wrote an article that was published in a magazine about the power of wind energy.

One exercise you might try is the word game. Begin with one word and just list subjects that have something to do with that word. I like to start with colors. For example YELLOW might lead to other words like SUN which leads to PLANETS or SUN SCREEN or SOLAR ENERGY. Or YELLOW could lead to DAISIES or FLOWER GARDENS or WHEAT or BUMBLE BEES or RARE COINS. Then these words might lead to other subjects like HOW DO BEES INFLUENCE FOOD CROPS? Or WHERE COULD YOU FIND PIRATE TREASURE?

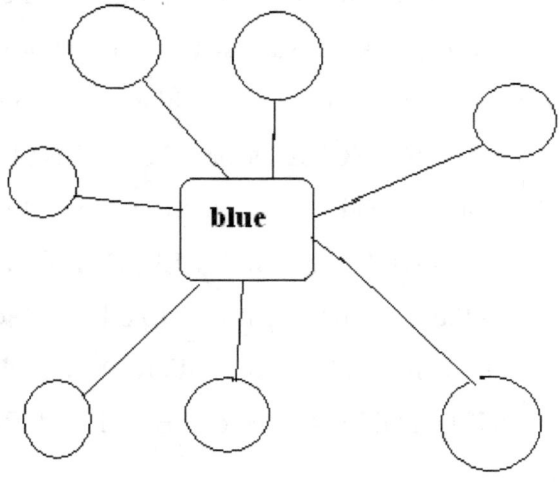

Let me help you with this. BLUE could remind you of SKY or WATER. Those words could make you think about SKY DIVING (Where can someone go to sky dive?), CLOUDS (Describe the different clouds we see.), AIRPLANES (Who first invented the airplane? Or How do airplanes get off the ground?), FISH (What is the best bait to use when bass fishing?), SCUBA DIVING (What is the process to get certified to scuba dive? Or describe the best places for scuba diving?).

Publishers are very interested in topics that are a new or an interesting twist on a popular subject. That means you need to look outside of the box. There are several ways to do this - first, check in a book store, library, or on-line to see how much is written on your topic, and second, go into your subject with a new and different approach. Editors will always reject a subject that has been written about endlessly by other authors. Give it a new twist.

If you have always wanted to write the next great novel that is near and dear to your heart, begin with something smaller. In fact begin several smaller projects. It gives you a better chance of getting published if you submit a short story or article first. Several published articles and stories give you credibility as a writer when you actually do submit that big writing piece you really want to see in print. So make a list of short topics you could easily write. Think about an article of about 500 - 1,000 words for this. Often new writers try to determine the length of an article by page length. But remember magazines and newspapers – and books – are not the typical 8 ½ X 11 size. So editors look at the word count rather than the number of pages.

_____

_____

_____

_____

_____

_____

_____

_____

_____

One thing to remember, when you present your idea to a publisher, it cannot simply be an IDEA. It must be completed before you send your query. Many new writers think they are able to send out an idea without actually writing the story. Then they receive an acceptance for something that is not actually in print. They find themselves struggling to complete that idea promised to a publisher— this can be real trouble! There is nothing to send. Please, please write your article, book, or story first. Then send out your query to the publishers. A great idea does not make a great manuscript! A "query" is a letter that presents your idea in an appealing and concise manner. We will discuss the query letter further in a later chapter.

_____

_____

_____

_____

_____

_____

_____

_____

_____

One way to avoid "Writer's Block" is by not "putting all your eggs in one basket". How is that for a few catch phrases? In other words, work on a few projects at the same time. That way when you find you are tiring or struggling with one, you are able to take a few days to work on another manuscript. When you return to the first project, you will feel refreshed and ready to tackle the issues formerly confronting you. Sometimes the project you thought was the most marketable just isn't, and the article you didn't think was great IS. It is always best to have "your fingers in a few pots." I carry a notebook to jot down ideas as they come to me during the day. That way you are not scratching your head later trying to remember that great thought you had that you knew you would never forget – but did!

_____

_____

_____

_____

_____

_____

As you begin your writing experience, ask yourself a few questions. Who are you as a writer? What do you want to accomplish? Define yourself. What is your vision? Everyone writes for a different reason. Some want to share their ideas or stories with others, some just feel fulfilled creatively when they write, and others are looking to market their writing and make a living. They are looking at the financial potential. Whatever your reason might be, define your purpose in writing.

_____

_____

_____

_____

_____

_____

_____

_____

_____

_____

_____

_____

FINDING THE RIGHT PUBLISHER

The first question I ask of the participants in my workshops is, "What is your genre?" Often times they don't know. Determine your writing category. First, is it book or short story, article or poem? Is it fiction or non-fiction? Many are confused by this question. If you have written the next great novel and it is based on fact but includes conversations you as a writer imagined might have happened, it is fiction. Many fiction stories are based on truth but include details and events that are made up. Take your genre a bit further. Are you writing a picture book, board book, middle grade chapter book, adult romance, or science fiction? These are just a few of the categories you must determine. When writing children's books, you must define what age group you are writing for and that does not mean two to ten. Children's age groups are divided into many specific groups. You may have to determine what the reading level for your book might be. Where does your writing fit?

When sending in a query to a publisher, or if you decided to self-publish, the first question asked is "Who is your reader?" If you are guessing at this question, delve further into what is required reading for different grade levels. If it is an adult novel, ask yourself who would most likely pick up your book? Who does your topic appeal to?

_____

_____

_____

_____

_____

_____

_____

_____

_____

_____

_____

_____

_____

_____

_____

_____

It is important to determine your genre before you begin to research publishers. Each publisher has specialty genres they publish. Many new writers think a publisher is a publisher. Not so! Each has certain areas in which they specialize. It is your task to research these to discover which fit your writing. Make a list of those most appropriate for your manuscript. Use a writer's guide or check websites to find those best for your project. One way to make a list of possible publishers would be to find other books similar in topic and readership to the one you are writing. Who is their publisher? Take those publishers and continue your research. What exactly do they publish? Do you like the look of the books they have on their list? Are they accepting queries or do they only take submissions from an agented author? WHEN do they accept queries?

As you research various publishers, do not think you are the exception to their rules. If a certain publisher only works with Canadian writers and you are not Canadian, do not put them on your list. If a publisher only publishes non-fiction, they will not publish your fantasy fiction novel. Each publisher will provide a list of guidelines for writers on their website. Carefully follow these guidelines. So if they require manuscripts to be 1,000 words, do not submit 2,000 words. If they require submissions only in November, do not send yours in December. FOLLOW THE GUIDELINES. Submit your manuscript in a form that is acceptable to that publisher. That may mean changing your format, the way you number your pages, the margins, the font, and the spacing. Publisher are very specific on their requirements. It gives you a better chance initially if they see you have followed the requirements.

When beginning your research, there are several areas you need to consider and note. What is the address, website, email, and editor's name? This knowledge shows the publisher when you address them personally that you have indeed done the research into their company. Note the % of freelancers used in a magazine, the word count requirements, submission guidelines including spacing and margins, and the topics published. What is their pay rate? Of course, the magazine or book publisher that pays the most seems to be the most appealing, but for a new writer, one that does not pay at all may be the best bet. Why? Because that may be the way to get publishing credits. Published writers are going to try for the big money. So if your goal is to get published, your first choice should be a magazine with no payment. Get a few published pieces under your belt before you submit the one manuscript you really want to see in print.

_____

_____

_____

_____

_____

_____

_____

_____

_____

_____

_____

_____

_____

_____

_____

If you have your list of possible publishers, take a look at their websites to see what books or articles they are currently publishing. Do you like the presentation? What do their covers look like, and what other topics are they publishing? If what they do does not appeal to you, and you just can't imagine your manuscript fitting their list, do not submit to this publisher.

Some writers make a list of 5 to 10 possibilities with the first on the list their top choice. Others make their list and put the best at the bottom of that list. Why? Because you can be sure you will receive rejections. It comes with the writing experience! So do not be discouraged when this happens. Some writers want to get feedback from those publishers they are not as excited about – get that rejection – before they submit to the publisher they really want to represent their manuscript. It allows them an opportunity to edit and redo their writing before submitting to the top choice.

Most publishers, whether magazine or book publishers, will require a query letter. A query letter is a one page presentation of your manuscript. The first paragraph is the hook — getting the reader to continue. It gets the publisher interested in what you are writing. The second and third paragraphs give the details of the writing such as word count and the reason the author wrote the manuscript. It also includes your qualifications for this writing project along with what is included in this correspondence (publishing history, resume, manuscript, writing samples, etc.). The query is actually more difficult to write than your manuscript because it is short and concise. Take your time to do an excellent presentation. Carefully consider your first paragraph and that opening sentence to make sure it is one that will catch the attention of the reader.

_____

_____

_____

_____

_____

_____

SAMPLE QUERY

Publisher's name

Address

Date

Dear Editor's name,

    First paragraph - intent is to get the publisher interested in your manuscript. Make them want to read more.

    Second paragraph - more details about manuscript such as word count, reason for writing this piece, and qualifications.

    Third paragraph - what is included in this correspondence and has this manuscript has been submitted to other publishers (simultaneous submissions). I always add a sentence explaining I am willing to make changes to accommodate their readership.

Your name

Contact info including address, email, phone number

I love researching publishers because their topics and needs always give me new fresh ideas for my next writing project. Each year I order a Writer's Market for magazines and books. I page through to highlight the subjects I feel would be an exciting writing idea. Now I have a list of writing goals for the year. Of course I could always add to these. What topics would you find interesting? (I always keep a CURRENT Writer's Market — information in this industry changes rapidly.) I had an experience when I began writing. I used a Writer's Market that was a few years old not realizing there might be changes in publishing. In the first set of ten queries I sent, I received seven back unopened. The publishers I had chosen had moved or were no longer publishing. I learned a valuable lesson. Stay current!

_____

_____

_____

_____

_____

When researching each publisher, make a note of their response times. Often new writers are impatient. Remember publishers are on a different time schedule than the writer. For example, when sending in an article on Halloween, you may need to submit it by March or before to fit into the publisher's yearly time frame. So when you send in a submission, note how long it will take before you will hear from the publisher. Dates of submissions should be documented so you are aware of when it was sent and when you can expect a timely response.

Writers keep track of their sent manuscripts and queries in different ways. Some use index cards, a computer spread sheet, or a simple notebook. Whatever your method might be for this process, make it easy and convenient for you. I find a notebook works best for me because I can easily have it open on my desk for daily notations. Anything that is complicated or hidden in a back closet will not be useful. You simply will not use it!

_____

_____

_____

_____

I've already mentioned the phrase "simultaneous submissions". What is this and why should a writer be concerned about this term? Simultaneous submissions means you are sending a manuscript to more than one publisher. Some publishers do not allow simultaneous submissions. So when sending them your manuscript, you must wait until they have determined a "yes" or "no" before sending it on to another publisher. This can be very time consuming. Other publishers may allow a simultaneous submission **if identified**. You would identify your intent to send the manuscript to more than one publisher in your query letter. Making a publisher aware of your intent may save you an uncomfortable moment if you receive two acceptances for the same manuscript. Exciting, but uncomfortable!

Always send your manuscript in the best condition possible. Some writers feel they should be able to send a manuscript with misspellings or in a confusing format. They think the editor will look past the sloppiness. They won't. Send a query and manuscript that is top quality and very neat. If you are questioning the format for your manuscript, check a proper format for writing a paper in an English grammar book. Often people tell me they understand this suggestion and then show me a manuscript that is far from an acceptable presentation. I've even had teachers show me a manuscript in an unacceptable form.

_____

_____

_____

_____

_____

_____

_____

_____

_____

I have mentioned several terms in connection to publishers: query, resume, outline, publishing history, synopsis, and writing samples. What are these? A query is a one page letter presenting your manuscript. A resume is your background including education and employment. An outline is a short list of what is presented in your manuscript. Publishing history lists the articles, stories, or books you have had published, when and where. A synopsis is a detail of your story and what happens throughout until conclusion. A writing sample may be requested by certain publishers to see if your writing style is compatible to their publication. It may or may not be a sample that has already been published. That depends on the requirements and requests found in the publisher's guidelines. How would you best describe these terms in your own words?

Query_____

Resume_____

Outline_____

Publishing History_____

Synopsis_____

Samples _____

Believe it or not, the very thing we fear — the rejection letter — may be a very effective learning tool for the writer. It gives insight into what works and what does not. For that reason, when selecting publishers make two or three lists. The first group, of course, should be your top choices. You are hoping for acceptance immediately. The second and third groups are those you will send your query to when you have received the rejections from the first group. The rejections will help you revise your query and possibly your manuscript to better fit the needs of the publisher and the reading audience. I've explained previously that some writers choose to send to the last publishers on the list first and save their top picks for last after receiving the first rejection. This allows them to edit and revise their manuscript. It is certainly up to you as to the strategy you choose.

_____

_____

_____

_____

_____

_____

One question most publishers will ask in regards to your manuscript is "Who is your market?" You need to determine who you expect your reader will be. And the answer to that question is not, "Everyone!" Then they will ask you if there are similar books or publications on your subject. Always be aware of your competition. Check with a library or bookstore to see what has already been written on your topic. Go on-line to pull up similar books or articles on your subject. Know who you are up against and what makes your idea unique. What does make your idea unique? That is what the publisher will ask.

_____

_____

_____

_____

_____

_____

_____

_____

_____

_____

SHOW ME THE MONEY

For some people looking to move into a writing career, the prospect of being a freelancer and therefore, self-employed may be confusing. It is not the usual job with the paycheck at the end of the week. Begin this new adventure by keeping very detailed records: what did you send out and to whom, what did you sell and for how much, and when can you expect to get paid. Of course, always keep track of the dates for everything. You think you will remember, but you won't. I keep a bound folder with a copy of each published article along with the cover of the magazine. We think we will remember each piece, but a few sold articles can quickly compound into many sales. Keep a record of EVERYTHING.

_____

_____

_____

_____

_____

_____

As a self-employed writer, you need to be aware not just about numbers regarding writing submissions but also about finances. Keep track of sales, expenses to deduct on your taxes, and sales tax. Sales tax is a concern for those writers who sell their own books whether they are published by a traditional publisher or self-published. Make sure you check with your state on regulations and register for a sales tax identification number.

If you are not familiar with the financial obligations of being self-employed, check with an accountant. Some states require you file income taxes quarterly or even monthly if you are self-employed. Also check on what is considered a deductible expense for you. These change yearly. So stay updated on the changes in tax regulations.

_____

_____

_____

_____

_____

_____

_____

_____

Writing is just like any other career. It takes training to learn the writing business. In order to learn what is important about this career, you must take classes, read books, study, attend workshops, and learn more. It is a never ending process especially now with this industry quickly changing. Book and magazine publishing is affected by technology and on-line publishing. It is affected by the closing of bookstores and libraries as well as the introduction of the Kindle, Nook, and ipad. So always continue to educate yourself about the craft. Take workshops and join support groups to learn the latest trends. Stay in contact with other writers. I subscribe to several publication dedicated to the writing industry and find these to be very helpful with issues and questions.

_____

_____

_____

_____

_____

_____

_____

Study the terms of publishing. Just what does this all mean? All rights, first rights, one time rights, second rights, kill fee. Learn the language of publishing so when you do land that big contract, you are aware of what your rights are regarding your manuscript. If you receive a contract and do not understand the terminology, take it to a lawyer that specializes in writers' contracts for clarification. Remember, you may always negotiate terms on the contract. So make a list of what may be of importance to you. Payment rates, royalties, advances, and character or photo property may be areas to consider.

All Rights:

First Rights:

One Time Rights:

Second Rights:

Kill Fee:

Royalties:

Advances:

Flat Fee:

Work-for-hire:

Be careful of contracts that indicate the publisher will have "all future rights". That means they may have rights to publishing changes in the future that we are unaware of at this point in time. Who knows what technology will be invented? A few years back we had no idea there would ever be a Kindle or Nook. It almost seemed impossible ten years ago but is quite ordinary today.

_____

_____

_____

_____

_____

_____

_____

_____

_____

_____

_____

_____

_____

Although we generally think of contract language for book deals, some magazines may also have a writer sign a contract. This contract is usually not quite as long and involved but may ask for a "non-compete clause". This may mean you are not able to write for a competitor. Think about this condition if you have a specific topic you would like to write about. It may limit who you are able to submit your writing to. Unless you have a wonderful relationship with the publisher you are signing this contract with, think about the implications it may have for your future as a writer. Book publishers may also require they have first option on your next book manuscripts if it is in a genre they publish. Are you happy with your relationship? Would you consider publishing with this company again?

_____

_____

_____

_____

_____

_____

_____

_____

Payment for writing can vary greatly depending on what is written and who is publishing that writing. There are some magazine and newspaper publishers that do not pay at all. Why would this be a good thing? A writer just starting out with no publishing history may want to get a few pieces published before sending on an important piece for payment. Other terms to understand are: flat fee, advance, royalty, payment per word, payment on acceptance, and payment on publication.

Always keep track of what your payment agreement is and when you can expect a check. There are times I have had to follow up on payments I was to receive only to discover they were missing a critical piece of information needed to send that check. Follow up on the money. You may write and receive acceptance for a manuscript one year and not expect payment until the following year. It is crucial to follow-up on payments due.

Never think you will make a living by publishing one book. Writing involves many published books or articles. Look at the whole picture and plan several writing projects. These will begin to accumulate to give you a viable part-time or full-time writing career. This may mean looking into other options such as editing, teaching, and staff writing. Look outside the box for areas you may not have considered such as movie or book reviews, newspaper columns, greeting cards, puzzles and poems. Many writers have found these areas bring in a great deal of income. Find your niche! What really works for you? What do you find is easiest and most rewarding for you?

There was one writer who found he had a talent for writing greeting cards. He would carry around note cards and jot down a sentence or two as thoughts came to him. When he had accumulated several cards, he would send them into a card publisher. They would send him a check for those they liked and return the rest. He made quite a good living by doing what came easy for his talents. Others would certainly not find this to be an easy writing assignment.

Even if you work with a traditional publisher, it is important to promote your own work. This may be in the form of book signings, interviews with local or national television or news shows, newspaper articles, or bylines in other publications. Do not be afraid to promote yourself. Call libraries or book stores to make sure they are carrying your book or magazine. Tell family and friends about your writing. Get out there and stand on your soap box about a special published piece or book. You are your own best form of advertising. Do not think writing does not entail selling. It is all selling starting first with the query to a publisher or agent. You are immediately selling your writing. Then you are again selling when your manuscript is finally published. Now you are selling your reader. I personally put together media packets for my books to send out to newspapers, television, and bookstores. It works! You need to be your own best fan.

As a self-employed person, you are also your own boss. That means you may write about what you choose, send out to whomever you choose, and give yourself a raise. Yes, that's right. Give yourself a raise. You may do that by beginning to submit to publishers who pay more. Generally, publishers offer a wide range of payment. They might say they pay for example from $100 - $300 for an article. That gives them the flexibility to offer more money to writers who they want to continue working with on a longer term basis. They are able to raise the rate of payment to someone with whom they have developed a relationship. It may be very worthwhile to develop that relationship with a publisher right from the start to reap the financial benefits later on.

You also give yourself a raise by sending out more manuscripts. The more manuscripts you write, send out, and sell is entirely up to you. That does not mean that you will sell more by sending more. No! If you are sending lots of manuscripts and receiving only rejections, you need to re-evaluate what and how you are writing. Ask someone to read your writing samples and make comments. What appeals to them and what doesn't? It is also best to ask someone who is not a relative or best friend. They may not always give you an honest answer (or maybe they will give a TOO honest answer! One you don't want to hear!). If you are receiving rejections, find out why. Attend a class or join a critique group for feedback. A little feedback can make a huge difference in your writing – and your income!

Finding a niche for your writing can mean money in your pocket. Take advantage of what you do best and develop your weaknesses into strengths. No one can be great at everything. So determine what you do well and what you need to improve upon.

Strengths:

_____

_____

_____

_____

Weaknesses:

_____

_____

_____

_____

_____

EDITING

After you have written an article, story or portion of a book, set it aside for a day before going back to edit what you have written. It allows your mind to move into a different place. When you reread something you have just written, it always sounds great because you are in the same frame of mind when you first wrote the words. But a day or two later, you may think, "What did I mean to say there?" You are in a different thought process that allows you to see something in a different mindset. Sometimes I read what I've written the day before and say, "Wow! That sounds great! I can't believe I wrote that." And other times I find myself saying, "What was I thinking?!"

_____

_____

_____

_____

_____

_____

When editing, read your writing out loud. Those of us who are fast readers see the content of the message rather than each individual word and may miss an "a" or "and" because we imagine it is there. Reading out loud means we must see each and every word as we go through the sentences allowing us to catch our small but important mistakes.

I know that one of my writing faults is spelling. My mother used to take letters I wrote home, correct the spelling errors, and send them back to me. I realize this problem and try to be very careful about spelling mistakes. We have become too accustom to helps like Spellcheck to catch our errors. Although I find Spellcheck to be a wonderful tool – especially for me! - Spellcheck is not perfect. It will not pull up a word if it is an actual word. For example, if you meant to use "your" and put in "you", it will not notify you of the mistake. So go through your manuscript carefully without assuming your computer program will catch the problems. My rule is, "When in doubt, look it up!"

_____

_____

_____

_____

_____

_____

_____

_____

_____

As you read through your manuscript, change any words you find yourself using over and over again. Duplicate words tend to make the writing boring. Also take out unnecessary words. I find I use the word "that" when it is not needed. So for me it is taking out ~~that~~ whenever possible. For example, "She said that it was important." If I take out "that", it becomes cleaner. "She said it was important." Much better.

_____

_____

_____

_____

_____

_____

_____

_____

_____

_____

_____

_____

_____

Writers are different. Many writers write long cumbersome sentences and when editing must cut out the unnecessary. Others write bare bones. They put down the most important parts of the story and when editing must go back and fill in — fatten the story a bit by adding more details. Which kind of writer are you? The cutter or the fattener?

_____

_____

_____

_____

_____

_____

_____

_____

_____

_____

_____

_____

_____

_____

_____

To make an article or story more interesting, make your sentences different lengths. Some writers use "run on sentences" — sentences that go on and on forever. I once worked for a man who wrote his own advertisements for the product he invented. He could write one sentence that took up one whole page of advertising. I offered to edit his writing, but he felt he wrote extremely well . . . Don't make this mistake in your writing. Vary your sentence length. Some sentences may be longer and others short and to the point. It makes the writing more interesting.

Vary the start of your sentences. Sometimes begin with a noun and then start the next sentence with a phrase. It makes reading so much nicer. I was working with one writer on her manuscript and discovered she began each sentence with an "ing" word. When I pointed this out to her, she was surprised. It was something she hadn't noticed before. Check your writing for such habits. Starting sentences the same way is very common. Vary the start of your sentences for a smoother read. I always say, if a reader is distracted by the writer's writing style, they miss the story or the point of the article. Get your point across without distracting writing habits.

_____

_____

_____

_____

_____

_____

_____

_____

Just like the first paragraph of a query letter draws the editor into reading on, the opening paragraph of your book or article must draw in the reader. It is the hook of your writing. Start with something that catches the attention and makes the reader want to read more. When writing a book, a great writer does this with each chapter opening. They also end each chapter with a reason to continue to the next page. It is sort of a cliff hanger in book form. Hint, imply, or give a brief glimpse into what is going to happen. It makes the story so much more interesting. Always remember when writing, if you have no problem, you have no story. Story is based on conflict — an issue to be dealt with or resolved.

Check on punctuation. Writers are always unsure of when to put in that comma and when to leave it out. How should the sentence end? If you are unsure, look up punctuation rules. Proper punctuation makes a huge difference in the way a story or book is read. It is also very distracting to a reader when writing is not properly punctuated. Please, if you are not sure, look it up. Also check on the proper use of some of the shorter words such as "to", "two", and "too". We all misuse these even when we know the difference. I always tell the story of a response I received from a school superintendent after I sent him a thank you e-mail. He responded with, "Your welcome." If you are reading this and don't understand what is wrong with the sentence, look it up! Remember, this was from a school superintendent! We all make mistakes.

When do you use each of these similar words?

to, too, two:

there, their, they're:

who's, whose:

its, it's:

accept, except:

capital, capitol:

where, wear:

whether, weather:

for, four, fore:

weigh, way:

your, you're:

reed, read:

ad, add:

air, err, heir:

ant, aunt:

I, eye:

bear, bare:

be, bee:

beet, beat:

here, hear:

bored, board:

by, bye, buy:

sent, scent, cent:

past, passed:

cite, site, sight:

course, coarse:

Rules for commas:

1) **To separate a series.**

   It was red, black, and blue.

2) **To separate two independent clauses.**

   The shirt was red, and the pants were blue.

3) **To separate an independent phrase.**

   Although the shirt was red, it was small.

4) **When using a parenthetical element (added information that can be removed and the meaning of the sentence does not change.)**

   The red shirt, in the corner, was small.

5) **To separate adjectives. Only use if the adjectives can be separated with the use of "and" or "but".**

   The small, red shirt was in the corner.

6) **To set off a quote.**

   He said, "That is my red shirt."

7) To set apart a contrasting phrase.

This, not that.

8) To avoid confusion.

Inside the red shirt is in the corner.

Inside, the red shirt is in the corner.

9) **Separate dates.**   June, 10, 2014

Separate city and state. Minneapolis, MN.

Separate name and title. John Smith, President

Separate numbers. 1,124

10) **Never separate a subject from its verb.**

Wanting to wear his red shirt was important to him.

When in doubt about punctuation, look up the rules for usage. Commas can be especially frustrating. When you have determined the correct use of commas and other punctuation, be consistent in your use.

Carefully check your verb tenses. If you begin telling your story in the past tense, you can't insert a sentence in the middle that is in the present tense. Ask yourself from what perspective is this story told — past, present or future? Then remain consistent. The same is true for who is telling the story. Are you telling this in the first person — your point of view — by saying "I", or are you telling this in the third person? If you begin through the eyes of one character, it may be difficult to change to another character's viewpoint. Some authors will write one chapter as told by one character and the next from someone else. Be careful. I read one manuscript told by the main character when suddenly one paragraph was inserted from the viewpoint of another person. It was just one paragraph! That made the flow very confusing. So carefully check your verbs and your story perspective.

When I speak to writers about the proper format for submitting in a manuscript, they all nod their heads as if they know just what I am saying. Then I look at their presentation and realize they have no idea what proper formatting is for a manuscript. Always follow the guidelines required by the publisher, but generally most will expect a Word document with 12 point font in Times New Roman double spaced. Some will give other instructions as well such as margin requirements. Follow what is expected. Some may have a detailed inch requirement for the placement of the title on the page, etc. Many will tell you how to number the pages. The two most common requirements for this would be a page number centered on the bottom of the page or in the upper left corner with the author's name and title of the manuscript on each page. Many book publishers receiving longer length manuscripts may require the name and title on each page.

_____

_____

_____

_____

_____

Here is a sample format for a manuscript:

Author's name
Address
Phone
Email

Date   Word count

Manuscript Title

Body of the manuscript. . . . .

_____

_____

_____

_____

_____

_____

_____

_____

_____

_____

_____

If you noticed, the sample for manuscript formatting included a space for word count. Generally the accepted wording of this is "About _____ words" even if you know the exact number of words in your article. Most publishers will give you either a specific word count requirement or an approximate length. When specific, follow the requirement. It is usually acceptable to have a 10% leeway either shorter or longer than the requirement. If the word count is 1,000 words, please do not think your article of 2,000 words will meet the rules. You are not the exception to the rule! Follow the guidelines.

Also notice in the sample format the "Body of the manuscript. . ." is indented. It is generally accepted that each paragraph is indented without extra spacing between paragraphs.

_____

_____

_____

_____

_____

_____

_____

Be consistent. If you begin to capitalize certain terms or words in your manuscript, follow through with your rule throughout. Let's talk about names. When you refer to "my mom" or "my sister" in a story, it is not capitalized. But if you use the word as a name, for example, "I told Mom I would do it.", you are using "Mom" as the person's name. It should be capitalized. If you write out your numbers, then always write them out. Don't use "10" in one place and "ten" in another. If you spell a name one way in the first sentence, don't change the spelling further down in the story. Be consistent with whatever rule you are following.

FINISHING YOUR PROJECT

We all reach a point in writing when we just can't get that manuscript finished! How can you motivate yourself to finish and move beyond the procrastination stage? Begin by setting some goals for yourself. I use a pie — eight pieces in a circle with a different generic heading in each piece. The circle is significant because when we have problems or issues in one of our "pieces", it affects the entire pie and not just that "piece". The eight headings I use for goal setting are: Spiritual, Career, Financial, Health/Fitness, Relationships/Family, Education, Recreation/Hobby, and Environment. Under each heading, I set five goals — three short-term and two long-term. Without the short-term goals, we never reach the long-term goals. They are the stepping stones to what we really want to achieve. I try to review and renew my goals every three to six months. Goals are the road map to our destination. Writing them down commits us to those goals. People who visualize where they want to be usually achieve what they desire in a faster more direct route.

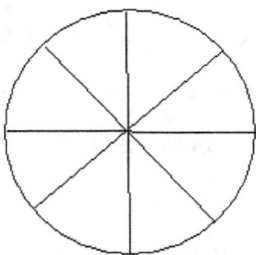

SPIRITUAL:

_____

_____

_____

_____

_____

CAREER:

_____

_____

_____

_____

_____

FINANCIAL:

_____

_____

_____

_____

_____

HEALTH/FITNESS:

_____

_____

_____

_____

_____

RELATIONSHIPS/FAMILY:

_____

_____

_____

_____

_____

EDUCATION:

_____

_____

_____

_____

_____

_____

RECREATION/HOBBY:

_____

_____

_____

_____

ENVIRONMENT:

_____

_____

_____

_____

_____

WRITING GOALS

One goal for a writer that encourages completion of a writing project is to set a writing schedule. Pick your time or days to write, and determine when and for how long you will be writing. Creating a writing habit can be very helpful. Remember it takes a bit of time to establish a new habit, so be patient with the process.

One of my writing friends decided to get up early each day to write. He set aside his writing time for 4:30 each morning for an hour or two. I'm sure that early hour of the day was not pleasant in the beginning, but soon he discovered when he had something that interfered with that schedule, he missed his writing time. He had created a habit that was as natural for him as brushing his teeth.

_____

_____

_____

_____

_____

_____

_____

A great goal for the Environment category is to create a space for yourself to write. It is so much easier to feel comfortable and begin to write when you are in an atmosphere that is conducive to creativity.

I find if I have a space where I have all of my tools set up to write, I will sit down and do it. But if I have to take out what I need and put it back afterward, I am not as likely to sit down in the first place. I can find so many excuses when the place I write is not easy to use.

Many find that a calm, stress-free environment provides a comfortable writing opportunity. If you find distractions from noises, other people, climate, technology (TV, radio, etc.) hamper your productivity, then create a space that gives you an environment that allows you to concentrate on your writing projects more completely.

_____

_____

_____

_____

_____

_____

Along with setting writing goals for yourself, set deadlines. Give yourself a time frame in which to work. You will find publishers give out lots of deadlines. They are also very eager to work with writers who adhere to those deadlines. I always finish and submit my assignments ahead of the assigned deadline to allow time for editing and changes if need be. Because I am always so dependable, I have received many additional assignments from editors who appreciate my punctuality. I love to hear an editor or publisher say, "You are so easy to work with!"

If you need a little jumpstart to complete a writing project, take a class, read a self-help book, or ask for help from a fellow writer. Use the tools available to you to give yourself additional motivation. We all need a little boost from time to time. Join a writers' support group for a weekly (or monthly) pump up. As with any career, additional research and information always gives a different perspective. Joining a class or writers' group is an excellent goal for the Education category.

_____

_____

_____

_____

_____

_____

_____

_____

_____

_____

_____

No matter what you are doing, whether it is writing or something else, you will always do better when feeling your best. That may mean getting enough rest, healthy eating, and exercise. So under the Health/Fitness pie piece, reviewing your lifestyle for a few changes toward healthier living can greatly help with your motivation and productivity in your writing. Setting health related goals not only improves the way you feel, but what you do.

_____

_____

_____

_____

_____

_____

_____

_____

_____

_____

_____

_____

_____

_____

Find someone to edit your work. I really recommend not asking a good friend or relative. They will always tell you how wonderful your writing is (unless you have the negative relative who never finds anything good about anything anyone else does!). They will love you and your work no matter how bad it might be. Ask someone else to edit for you to get honest feedback. You may have to pay a few dollars, but it is worth it. When submitting to an agent or publisher, however, never pay a "reader fee". They are compensated by representing someone who sells books and makes money from those books – not from charging to read a manuscript. But you may have to pay a minimal fee to someone who does editing before the manuscript is sent off. It is a good investment to receive honest feedback on your work.

_____

_____

_____

_____

_____

_____

Some writers edit and edit and edit . . . There is a point when you should stop editing and just accept that it is done. Remember, nothing is ever perfect. No matter how much you edit, there will always be something that can be changed to make it better. But if you don't move on to the next step, you won't have the opportunity to get to the publishing phase of writing. Accept that your writing is not perfect and move on. Go on to the next writing project.

I have found many writers say they want to publish a manuscript, but when it gets right down to accomplishing that goal, they drag their feet. There is always the fear that someone actually reading their work will find fault. Rejection is never comfortable. But remember nothing will be 100% accepted by everyone. There will always be a few critics in the group no matter what we do. That should not prevent a writer from the final publishing step. Move beyond the fear factor.

_____

_____

_____

_____

_____

Goals we make are changeable. They are not set in stone. So if something you are doing is not working, change it. Review your goals and revise them for any adjustments that may be needed. Don't keep hitting your head against the wall over and over again. Go in a different direction. It is all right to change. It is all right to revise a goal. Look outside the box for another perspective when you find yourself at a standstill.

TRADITIONAL PUBLISHING
OR
SELF-PUBLISHING?

A few years ago, I would never advise writers to try anything but a traditional publisher. Then I began to read about experiences by other writers who recommended self-publishing and decided to look into it myself. Self-publishing has become very popular recently and seems to be the future for many writers. Both paths have their pros and cons. So take a look and decide for yourself which way is best for you. Maybe both are good choices.

Just a brief explanation, this section is related to BOOK publishing. While it is possible to self-publish your own magazine or newspaper, right now the self-publishing question is more controversial in the book publishing field.

_____

_____

_____

_____

_____

_____

Traditional Publisher

Pros:

Many writers like to focus on the writing portion of this business and leave the promotion and formatting to the publisher. The traditional publisher will design your cover and format the interior of your book as well as provide media attention. This is not to say you will not do some of the promotion — you will! But you need not do as much of this with a traditional publisher. The publisher will also suggest editing ideas for you. Of course, the traditional publisher is still accepted as a standard of excellence in the writing field. Because anyone can self-publish, readers may still feel the quality work will be produced by a traditional publisher who weeds out the writers who don't quite make the mark.

Many books are now purchased on-line or in an e-book format, taking away business from the traditional bookstore. Many of the smaller bookstores are going out of business due to this trend. In addition, many of the traditional bookstores are a little reluctant to carry books in their establishments from a self-publishing company because the return policy for unsold books is not the same as for a traditional publisher. This is something to consider when weighing the potential for traditional publishing vs. self-publishing. Where is your market? Is it through the bookstore or with the on-line reading market. It will be interesting to see where this trend moves in the future. Will the corner bookstore become non-existent in the future?

With the new trends in on-line book purchases and self-publishing potential, traditional publishers are becoming a bit more selective in their book lists. Unfortunately, it helps to have a well-known name on the book. A movie star or political figure with a new book will always become a bigger seller initially than an unknown first time author with a great story. That is the reality!

_____

_____

_____

_____

_____

_____

Cons:

Basically there are two negatives about the traditional publisher. First, you may not have as much say in what the finished project will look like. Some writers really want to have their fingers in all areas of their writing project because it is so much a part of them. Second, you must also share the profits from the sale of your book. So while using a traditional publisher may get your book more exposure, and therefore, more sales, you must split the money with the publisher. Weigh the potential here. More sales and less money from those sale, or fewer sales and more money from the sale of each book. Which gives you more potential financially?

Time! One of the biggest objections for a traditional publisher is the amount of time it takes for the entire process. First, it takes time after the initial query to find a publisher to accept the manuscript and sign a contract. Second, it often times takes one to two years after the contract is signed to see your book in print. Many authors find this long span of time to complete the project to be a surprise and a detriment to the publishing appeal of the traditional publishing process.

Self-Publishing

Pros:

A few years ago, the self-publishing companies required writers to heavily invest in publishing a book. The writer had to come up with a bit of cash up-front to finance the printing of the books and guarantee a large quantity would initially be printed. Today however, self-publishing does not require ANY up-front cash. The printing is done on demand and feels much like a traditional publisher would print a book. The writer, although able to hire someone from the publishing company to format, edit and design the cover, also has the option to do this work himself/herself. The writer who really wants to get personal with a manuscript is now able to do all of the designing, formatting, cover, and promotion of that book. There are those who really benefit from this. Those who are teaching a class or speaking at seminars and want to provide a book for that event is very able to do this without splitting profits with a publisher. So there is the possibility with work to make more money from this option.

There are authors who do not want to wait for a book to get picked up by a traditional publisher. It can be a timely process sometimes. Then again, there are authors who will never be picked up by a traditional publisher because their writing needs work or might be about a controversial topic that a traditional publisher hesitates to chance. These authors find self-publishing the only way to go.

An author can write, format, and get a book published through self-publishing in a relatively short amount of time. Some can take a manuscript, do the formatting, upload the files to a publisher and see the book in print and available to a reader within twenty-four hours! The time element can be very satisfying to a writer educated in the formatting process. It is a relatively simple procedure.

_____

_____

_____

_____

_____

_____

_____

Cons:

When you must wear all of the hats — writer, editor, designer, formatter, and promoter — it can be overwhelming and time consuming. Not many people are able to do it all pieces of a project with excellence. This is a decision a writer who selects this path must decide. Of course you can choose to have someone else do some of those pieces for you – at a cost, of course! But the cost may be relatively small for the end result. If you are not a computer tech guru, hire one to do your formatting. If you need editing, hire someone to do that as well. If you have no creative talent, hire an artist to do your cover. If you are not media savvy, hire a promotional expert to schedule events, book signings, and media presentations to promote the sale of the book. It is a matter of business. And business is best when you have others do what they do best. The project takes on a whole new life! It can be a very enjoyable process.

_____

_____

_____

SELF-PUBLISHING TIPS

Let's first look at the basic appearance of your book. If you are writing your manuscript in Word, you must first realize the way you present your book is exactly the way it will look in print. The magic book fairy will not come along and zap your book into an acceptable form. You must do that yourself. First, determine the size of your book. Most books are not the standard 8 ½ X 11 that Word uses (not to say it can't be). There are several Standard sizes as well as several Custom sizes to choose for your completed book.

<u>Standard Trim</u>
5.5 X 8.5
6 X 9
6.14 X 9.21
7 X 10
8 X 10
8.5 X 8.5
8.5 X 11

<u>Custom Sizes</u>
5 X 8
5.06 X 7.81
5.25 X 8
6.69 X 9.61
7.44 X 9.69
7.5 X 9.25
8.25 X 6

When you have determined what size will work for your book concept, resize your book in Word to see how many pages your manuscript will now be when printed. Remember when resizing to consider the margins as well. The print may need a different sides, top and bottom adjustment to look the way you want when printed. The number of pages will determine the print cost of your manuscript into book form. So if you have a thousand page novel, you will have quite a hefty print cost (especially if you want the interior to be in color rather than in black and white!). You will also select what price you will be charging for your book, and this is based on the cost to print. So if your epic novel costs too much, your reader will not purchase your book. Set a few price points you would like to use as a guideline so you can make any changes while editing to fit that framework. I noticed with one self-publisher the authors were pricing their books very high. While a higher price will give you more money from a sale, it may also limit how many sales you have. Weigh the pros and cons of each — higher price and more royalty or lower price and more books sold. Which works for you?

With self-publishing, the author has the option of selecting full color interior or black and white. (The cover of course will most likely be in color!). When making this decision, consider that the full color is of course more expensive to print. So if you have illustrations, consider whether they will be effective in black and white. This will keep your print cost down and allow you to sell your book for a reasonable price. If you need the full color, you may consider cutting the number of print pages. Fewer pages to print equals lower cost for each book.

_____

_____

_____

_____

_____

_____

Your cover, both front and back, will also need to fit the size you have chosen for your print page. After you have completed your writing and formatting, determine the number of pages your book will be including title page, copyright page, introduction, table of contents, and any blank pages needed to allow your book to open to a first page on the right side. These are all included in your page count. Then submit this count to your publisher along with the page size to print out a cover template. The template will give you the dimensions you will work with to design your cover. This template will give space for the front cover, back cover, and spine. Using a publishing program such as Publisher or GIMP, insert your cover designs along the template guidelines and determine how you want your spine to look. Then save this as a Word file and again as a PDF file. The PDF file is the one you will upload to your publisher's site. The inside portion of your manuscript should also be saved as a PDF file and uploaded.

The interior of the book should begin with two Word files – one for the introduction pages and one for the interior numbered pages. You do not want your title page, disclaimer/copyright page, dedication and Table of

Contents to be numbered. You want the page numbers to begin with your manuscript on page one. Unfortunately, Word does not allow at this time (maybe in the future) to number your pages starting at a certain point in the document. It just numbers them all! So take your part 1 and save it in a PDF format. Then take your part 2 and save it in another PDF file. Join the two files together, and you will have the numbered pages where you want them to be. This merged file in PDF format is the one you will upload to your publishing site.

You may change and re-change your cover and your interior as much as you like within the publishing process. But the one constant is the title you use and ISBN number (International Standard Book Number) must remain the same. That number is the one assigned to your title. So when selecting your title, make sure it is one you want to keep. It is also a good idea to Google your title to see if it comes up as one already taken by someone else prior to making your final decision.

I like to use Createspace for my self-publishing process. One of the reasons is it is owned by Amazon.com so the book is readily available after publication to the Amazon consumer. I can also get a free ISBN number assigned to my title immediately. If you would like to purchase your own ISBN number, you would do so through Bowker. An ISBN number is the identification number assigned to a specific book that you find on the copyright page of each book. It coordinates with the barcode on the back cover of the book located in the lower right corner.

After your title has been assigned the ISBN number (usually there will be two with starting numbers 10: and 13:), copy these numbers to your copyright/disclaimer page usually located on the back of the title page. Remember, the way you view your manuscript when completed is the way it will look when in print. You are the one who puts EVERYTHING into the book. The publisher does not do this.

After you upload your cover and completed interior, you will be allowed to view the proof of your book with the on-line viewer and/or a hard copy version before you accept the manuscript as ready for publishing. Before you accept your proof, you may find yourself making changes. Maybe a page doesn't quite line up the way you expected or a picture doesn't print as well as you would have liked.

Maybe some of the pages are not on the side of the page you expected and you need to add or remove blank pages to make the format look the way you want. You may upload new files after you have made the corrections. Createspace also allows you to select the areas of distribution for your book (the United States, worldwide, libraries, bookstores, on-line, etc.) as well as your purchase price. The price must be over the cost of printing as well as one that reflects the price of distribution. You will be able to determine how much you as the author will make on each book purchase depending on the venue of the sale. Some sites will allow you a larger percentage of the book profit.

E-BOOK FORMATTING

When typing and planning the hard copy of your book, consider what you may need to do to convert this book to an e-book. At this time, the various popular e-books are in different formats. It would be so much easier for writers who would like to format their manuscripts themselves if this would change in the future. I predict it will. While I do not profess to be any type of expert at all in computers, formats, and programs, I did format several of my books myself — with the help of a few of my college aged children I had to beg for assistance. Our generation is not as knowledgeable as the younger generation who has grown up with the technology of today. It is not an easy process, I will confess. Some of the type and spacing of the Word file does not easily transfer to e-book format. These things are quickly changing, and the transition is becoming easier and easier. I have noticed some symbols do not transfer, and it is not advisable to use your Tab key to indent paragraphs as it doubles the spacing in the transfer. I hand tab when typing the original manuscript for an easier transfer.

I use the Kindle format owned by Amazon because it is automatically uploaded for sale by Amazon. While the self-publishing companies now offer to upload your hard copy manuscript to Kindle for free, I have found their formatting to be awkward and not a quality product. So I continue to do the formatting myself. The first thing to do is download a free Kindle previewer to your computer. This can be found on the KDP Select site. The previewer allows you to view your files in the different Kindle formats. Each format is a bit different in width, size, and quality, so it is always good to test each one before uploading the file to the KDP Select site for publishing.

First, your front cover (the one that is visible to the reader on Amazon) should be in a jpeg format. Convert your Word or your PDF file to the new format before uploading. The interior should be in HTML format (Mobi). When reformatting your Word document, you should save it as "Web Page, Filtered". The HTML file will change some of your font and your spacing. This can be frustrating and may require changes to your Word file.

Before saving your Word file to the HTML format, there are a few reformatting steps to take. Step one in reformatting is to take out all of your page numbers on your Word file and rejoin your part 1 and part 2 into one Word document. An e-book does not have pages. The reader may set the size of the font for their own reading taste making numbered pages unnecessary. Second, take out your ISBN number as it will not be the same one in the hard copy version. Next, move all of your text together with no spaces between pages. Now put in page breaks for chapters or between introductory pages so the HTML format and the

Kindle Previewer will acknowledge the spaces between print content. Double check your pictures and their spacing. Now save your file as "Web Page, Filtered" creating your HTML file. Upload this file to your Kindle Previewer and take a look. Does everything align properly? Do you like the formatting? If not, make changes to your file. I like to use a free program called SeaMonkey to change my HTML files. It allows me to move around pieces that do not seem to align properly, change font, and connect Table of Content chapters to the actual chapter itself. I continue to go back and forth between SeaMonkey and the Kindle Previewer until I find the formatting acceptable. Then upload the Mobi file created by the Kindle Previewer to the KDP Select website.

With both the e-book and the hard copy, you need to create an account on these websites. Be prepared to have several pieces of information available when you create your account: title of your book, a description of the book (usually a paragraph visible to the reader when they view your book/e-book on Amazon.com), keywords you want to connect with your book that allows the potential reader to pull up your title when looking for a certain subject, your credit card, and your banking information. Your credit card information allows you to purchase the proof and any other books you would like for yourself. The banking information and tax info (company, tax ID, and/or Social Security number) allows the publisher to PAY you for your royalties (your sales!) as well as send you your tax information at the end of the year. Yes, you should be making money on your book which the publisher files with the IRS, and you must declare your profits on your taxes. You are now a published author with income from your writing!

Remember, if you sell books yourself, you must also charge the sales tax specified by your state. Call your state sales tax department and find out what the process entails. You may have to create a sales tax number and file quarterly, monthly, or yearly depending on your state and your sales. In my state each area code has a different tax rate. So the amount charged would vary depending on where the book is sold.

_____

_____

SHOULD YOU FIND AN AGENT?

People usually ask about finding an agent. While many writers will tell you it is important to have an agent, I am a little reluctant to advise a new writer to immediately find an agent. The process to find an agent is about the same as finding a publisher. You must submit your query, manuscript, and publishing history/resume to an agent just as you would to a publisher. There are some genres that really do need an agent. Adult fiction novelists will find an agent does generally have more connections to some of the larger publishing houses. Also consider if you use an agent, you once again split your profits with another group, and you are already splitting your money with the publishing company if using a traditional publisher. An agent is great for better connections and should be able to get a better contract. If the agent doesn't do this, then they are not needed. The best agents are already representing enough writers that they do not need anyone new in their stable. So most new authors looking for an agent will most likely find a newer agent as well. This is one area you might want to consider the pros and cons before jumping into. SCBWI (Society for Children Book Writers and Illustrators) offers lists of agents on their website for their members. They also provide legal answers and connections to illustrators, writing contests, and grants. I highly recommend looking into membership in the SCBWI.

Just a quick last note on agents. If they charge a reading fee, find someone else. Be very careful to find an honest and reputable agent. There are many who are not. However, a positive relationship with an agent can be very productive and save the author many hours of searching for a suitable publisher for a project as well as creating more opportunity for success.

_____

_____

_____

_____

_____

_____

_____

_____

COMMENTS ON OTHER TOPICS

Writers designing picture books always ask about illustrations and illustrators. You do not need to provide an illustrator (or illustrations) if you are submitting copy to a publisher. In fact, most publishers recommend an author not do so unless they are also an artist. Publishers have favorite illustrators they like to use for their books. If you are an artist, you may also consider submitting a portfolio or sample illustrations to publishers to keep on file for use in their upcoming book projects with other authors.

_____

_____

_____

_____

_____

_____

_____

_____

_____

_____

_____

Picture book writers should also understand what a "mock-up" or dummy is. Picture books are usually printed in a format that looks like a page folded in half. That means there are certain standard page counts used in this process. Generally they are 16, 32 or 48 page formats. Remember, included in this page count is the title page, copyright page, and any dedication page as well as blank pages. Many publishers will request you submit a mock-up indicating where you want your copy and your illustrations.

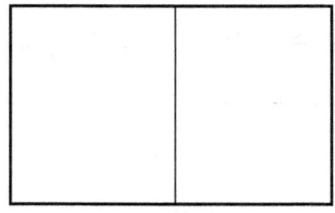

This is a sample mock-up page. If you take 8 of these pages and fold them, you would have the 32 page format. On each page indicate where you want your words and pictures.

_____

_____

_____

If you are considering self-publishing a book, determine before you publish what your promotion plan will be. How will you get your book out in front of your readership? Currently writers are using several methods: Google and other search engines, Facebook, Pinterest, Linkedin, blogs, and Twitter. Most writers will also recommend having a website to promote their product(s). Have these options in place before you complete your publishing process so you are able to immediately send out information to your readers. That may mean establishing a following before you put out the book. Connect with a lot of people! Who do you think your readership will be?

Other items to consider are business cards, media packets, and fliers. You might consider contacting retail stores you think would be interested in displaying your book. Think outside the box on this one. For example, if you write about plants, consider offering your book for sale at greenhouses or florist shops. Having said this, please make sure you publish a hard copy at the same time as you put out an e-book. While e-books are gaining popularity among readers of all ages, you must have something physical in hand when promoting your book.

Most authors consider bookstores to be the best opportunity for their book and their sales, however, consider the bookstore will also want to make money. So you are going to give up a piece of your profit for the bookstore to carry maybe one or two copies of your book. There are other venues that may be more suitable for your book. Consider who your readership might be. For example, if you are writing for children, a children's toy store or clothing store might be a better place to present your product. One author I worked with wrote about vineyards. The book signings were scheduled for wine tasting in the vineyards listed in the book. Another of my workshop authors talked about local places in her young adult fiction story, so began to promote her book at the skating rink where the story took place. My Dancemaster mystery series does very well at dance competitions because it appeals to the dancers who attend these events.

So the best idea is to consider where your readership might better find your product. Think outside of the box and determine a financially easy plan – something that gives you the most profit. Invest your money and time wisely for a bigger payoff.

Although I don't like to show favoritism toward certain companies or products, I will tell you who I personally use for some of these areas. I recommend finding your own favorites as well.

Amazon.com

Bowkers

Barnes and Noble

Createspace (self-publisher owned by Amazon)

KDP Select (Kindle publisher)

Wordpress (for bloggers)

Goodreads

Vistaprint (FREE business cards and other supplies)

Facebook

SCBWI (Society for Children's Book Writers and Illustrators) a wonderful group for writers of all genres

www.writersbookstore.com They publish writer's market books both for books and magazines.

The Institute of Children's Literature A great place to take correspondence writing classes and workshops.

Register.com for websites

This list is only a start. There are many other places to consider in your promotion process. Ask other writers who they use for media services.

_____

_____

_____

_____

_____

_____

_____

_____

_____

_____

_____

_____

_____

_____

_____

_____

_____

_____

_____

In my workshops, I always tell writers to contact me with questions. So I will end with this as well — contact me! Happy writing and best of luck in your publishing process.

Charlene Torkelson

TCTork@msn.com

www.chartorkelson.com

Or find me on Facebook, Twitter, Pinterest or Linkedin.

www.ingramcontent.com/pod-product-compliance
Lightning Source LLC
Chambersburg PA
CBHW070210290526
45789CB00002B/962